IMAGINARY
TIMBER

IMAGINARY TIMBER

POEMS BY

James Galvin

DOUBLEDAY & COMPANY, INC.
Garden City, New York
1980

Library of Congress Cataloging in Publication Data

Galvin, James.
Imaginary timber.

I. Title.
PS3557.A444I4   811'.54
ISBN: 0-385-15776-2
Library of Congress Catalog Card Number 79-6746

for my father,
for Lyle VanWaning,
and Ray Worster.

Grateful acknowledgment is made to the publications in which the following poems first appeared:

Agni Review: "Fool's Errand"
The American Poetry Review: "Three Songs of the One-Man Band"
Antaeus: "Everyone Knows Whom the Saved Envy," "For Remembering How to Live Without You," "Navigation," "Cache la Poudre"
Antioch Review: "A Discrete Love Poem"
Columbia: "Ode to the Brown Paper Bag"
Crazyhorse: "Utah Ghost Town," "Getting a Word In"
Georgia Review: "A Man's Vocation Is Nobody's Business"
The Iowa Review: "Airbrush," "A Poem from Boulder Ridge," "Making Hay and Funerals," "Homesteader"
Ironwood: "To a Friend I Can't Find"
The Nation: "Notes for the First Line of a Spanish Poem," "News," "Something to Save Us," "The Stone's Throw," "The Longest Distance Between Two Points," "Lemon Ode," "Rosary of Conspiracies," "That Falling We Fall"
Ohio Review: "Fugue for a Drowned Girl"
Paris Review: "Sadness," "Snowlight"
Poetry Northwest: "The Snowdrift as a Wave"
Poetry Now: "Totem"
Seneca Review: "What I've Believed In"
Skywriting: "Fathers and Indians"
Toyon: "The Small Self and the Liberal Sky"
Water Table: "As If." "Hermits"
The last three stanzas of "Consideration of the Sphere" appeared in *The New Yorker* under the title "Devotions."
"Everyone Knows Whom the Saved Envy" appeared in *Pushcart* III.

I would also like to thank the National Endowment for the Arts for a grant that helped me to finish this book.

Contents

I

II

III

IV

I

NOTES FOR THE FIRST LINE OF A SPANISH POEM

We remember so little,
We are certain of nothing.
We long to perish into the absolute.
Where is a mountain
To spread its snowfields for us like a shawl?

You might begin,
The men who come to see me are not exactly lovers.
Or, *Seen at a distance the gazelle is blue.*
That's just your way of cheering me up.

You might begin,
The quality of the telegram is vulnerable.
Or even, *The spirit of the telegram is virginal.*
By now I am ravenous.

You might begin,
Nothing's more passionate than a train,
Entering an enormous depot,
Empty except for two lovers, irreconcilable,
Parting. Then,
No one's more visible than a blind man on the street.

Things that are that were never meant to be!
Terrible music!

The utter confusion of surfaces!
The first steps toward probability!
You might begin,

Near the edge of the mind, the mind grows defenseless,
Sleepy in the way it sees,
Like Columbus on the edge of the world.
It feels the grip of all it cannot grasp,
Like the blind man trying to stay out of sight.
Show me any object, I'll show you rust on a wave.

You begin,

Outside the mind, the snow undresses and lies down.

NEWS

These afternoons seem to occur more
In geologic time than in one's life.
Under the blue fresh snowfall,
Sandstone outcrops generate heat.
I count fifteen kinds of tracks,
Like runes, and nothing living.

Drifted snow, an ethered gauze,
Muffles the land, creaks under my skis,
Animals sleep among the roots,
Without doors, without dreams.
Seven miles for a phone
And even the wires have gone under.

Another day knowing nothing more
Than when I last saw you,
That stainless-steel shadow
Vigilant over your bed.
It followed you down the hospital halls,
Arms hung with surgical fruit.

I slide down the last drift to the house,
Slap my skis together.
A small avalanche, shaped like a continent,
Drifts off the roof and falls into a heap,
And some chinking falls from the eaves.

We each inhabit our own
Small flesh, our tract.
Each tries to keep his own
Doors from creaking, like news,
As each night slams shut, and each dawn opens
Like a sudden flow of blood from the mouth.

EVERYONE KNOWS WHOM THE
SAVED ENVY

It isn't such a bad thing,
To live in one world forever.
You could do a lot worse:
The sexual smell of fresh-cut alfalfa
Could well be missing somewhere.
Somewhere you'd give in to some impetuous unknown,
And then stand guilty, as accused, of self-love.
It's better not to take such risks.

It's not as if we had no angels:
A handful remained when the rest moved on.
Now they work for a living,
As windmills on the open range.
They spin and stare like catatonics,
Nod toward the bedridden peaks.
They've learned their own angelic disbelief.

The mountains still breathe, I suppose,
Though barely.
The prairie still swells under a few small churches.
They are like rowboats after the ship's gone down.
Everyone knows whom the saved envy.
Runoff mirrors the sky in alpine pastures;
Imagine how quickly one's tracks unbloom there.
This world isn't such a bad world.

At least the angels are gainfully employed:
They know where the water is,
What to do with wind.
I try not to think of those others,
Like so many brides,
So many owls made of pollen
Wintering in a stand of imaginary timber.

SOMETHING TO SAVE US

As far as we know there's nothing more to say
About being so small for our size,
Nothing, therefore, about parentage.

There's nothing to say about maritime sadness:
Immodest signals from unreachable islands,
Earthrise on the moon.

There's little to say about innocence:
We'd land on distant planets
Like flies on the anvil;

We'd abandon our unborn,
Those intervals crouched around us wherever we are.
We'd wish the self even smaller,

Though the self is already smaller
Than anyone suspects.
All we wanted was a roundness we could count on.

There's nothing to say about the history of resurrection,
The chronicles on incapacity,
Nothing about falsehood or humor.

We are like relatives after an execution:
We've said we are like our own worn clothes
Hung to dry without us;

We've said we are like the windows of our own house
Falling away all at once;
We take root in the sound of our own breaking.

If there were something more to say,
How would that save us—
Violets, parasol, easy rain?

LINES ABOUT THE RECENT PAST

In the recent past,
Always mad or dreaming,
Diminished by even a little distance,
I resemble everyone.

Is the wind dying? Is the spade willing?
I don't ask.

In the recent past weather is obsessive.
The sun is something complete
That sometimes looks away.

On their own good strength the cattle return
From all the long days of giving up their flesh.
Is this how we travel to the heart,
Like pollen back from the air?

I just want to say,
The past and the stiletto are shy by design.
It's unlikely that I'm mistaken in this.

They enter in a way less honest than true.

So much lowering of eyes!
In the recent past is the sleep of humility.

It's easy to belong in the world.

There are angels in the snow where birds have landed.

THE SNOWDRIFT AS A WAVE

for my mother

Consider this hour, this death.
It leans toward me. We touch.
It has a fragrance like burning lace.

Pitch-wood in the furnace:
The damned making love,
The drowned in their ships, tapping with wrenches.

The winter I was eight,
Snow drifted up twenty feet around our house.
We left the truck and snowshoed home.
Father brought his mother, bundled on my sled.

Had you stopped to rest,
To lean your arm against a tree?
Were you always so unhappy?

A sail billowing under the coals,
A seed waking in its pod.

I tunneled into that drift, made rooms,
Listened to the blizzard
As it made more waves like mine.
I had seen the sea once.

It opened its waves like drawers,
Repeating the name of something misplaced.
It searched the same drawers again and again.
It sounded like that snowstorm
Giving itself away.

SADNESS

Tonight in the Southwest
Sadness is disappearing

Tonight in splash marks
On boulders

In the streambed
Sadness is disappearing

On mesas
In processions

Of miner's candles
Like Hohokam

Returning from the gulf
With salt

Tonight in the eyes
Of the oldest lion

Stirring in our tracks
And in the heart

Of the cactus blossom
In the red spider

Knitting wheels
Humming to herself

In a voice like transparent thread
Sadness is disappearing

The maidenly lizard
In her sandstone room

In the dim light of a quartz lamp
Makes love to her shadow

Sadness is disappearing
Tonight in the desert

Like a drop of blood
On the map of the Southwest

And above us
A few in the dark audience

Smoking cigarettes

THE MEASURE OF THE YEAR

A canoe made of horse ribs tipped over in the pasture.
Prairie flowers took it for a meetinghouse.
They grow there with a vengeance.

Buck posts float across the flooded swamp
Where my father rode in and under.
Different horse.

He held her head up out of the mud
And said how he was sorry
Till they came to pull him out.

We found the white filly
On the only hard ground by the south gate.
He said she'd been a ghost from the start and he was right.

We covered her with branches.
There were things he had the wrong name for
Like *rose crystals*. Though

They were about what you'd think from a name like that.
He told us somewhere on Sand Creek Pass
Was a crystal that spelled our own initials

And we should try to find it.
We walked through sagebrush and sand currents, looking.
He said pasque flowers and paintbrush

Wait till Easter to grow,
Then they come up even with snow still on the ground.
I thought I'd seen that happen.

AIRBRUSH

The sky was an occasion
I would never rise to. I had my doubts.

Frost fell back into morning shadows of things.
Gateposts and evergreens had two shadows then,
One white and twice as cold
With half the heart and half again
Smaller.

Better than expected was good enough.
A man could say *mercy* and mean it.

There were daughters in whom fathers
Would be well pleased, sons
Not able to breed, mothers among the living.

Fields blew away and blew back in, painless.
Everybody died since everybody does, still

I have my doubts
And they have shadows, double.

A MAN'S VOCATION IS NOBODY'S BUSINESS

Overcome with humility in the American West,
Boys grew up incorruptible in old photographs.
In shirts without collars,
They stand next to the year's prize hog,
Thinking into the wind.

Taller than fathers or brothers,
The edges of kitchen doors
In sod houses
Recorded the ambitions of boys to grow

Tall enough to see more
Of the landscape as it took
Its turns for the worse.

From the top of a silo you could see
How the land had a hard time
Just holding up its fences,
Holding out for water, just holding
Back the sage and larkspur.

In eastern Colorado, old men and boys
Rode the fences together.
Once a year, in late summer,

They lifted the fence wires to the tops of cedar posts
For the tumbleweeds to blow under.

This is no secret.
The tumbleweed is a bristling genius
Bound for the edge of the world.

THE SMALL SELF AND
THE LIBERAL SKY

Perhaps you didn't realize
Anything can happen under a sky like this.

Never give in to surprise:

Not for mountains
Who turn under sheets and breathe in
Each other's green scent;

Not for the lights where nobody lives;

Not for blood-colored mushrooms
That rise up one after one like little presidents;

Not for the small self, afraid
It has misunderstood the question.

Oh it's prepared to answer anyway,
It has its array of modest affirmations
Like anyone. Just that—

So many years and something in the leaves
Does not fall.

I find young starlings in the lake's ice,
Their wings spread like death-flowers pressed in a book;

(21)

Find moths spawned in the woodshed
Like a winter's supply of blossoms.

It's just that I was looking for a world
To walk into empty-handed.

That's when I found you, female, shamelessly
Sailing toward me in your folded paper boat.

Don't deny it, please.
At night the self feels smaller
And water is scarce in parts of the mind.

The small self is obliged, therefore,
To take back everything
Anyone has ever said.

No one is allowed to speak now
But you

II

WHAT I'VE BELIEVED IN

Propped on blocks, the front half of a Packard car rides the
hillside like a chip of wood on the crest of a wave. It's part
of the sawmill. That Packard engine runs it, or did. The rest,
the belt, the Belsaw carriage and blade, stands aside in dis-
repair. Except for the pine seeds gophers have stashed in the
tailpipe, there's no sign of anything living. The gull-wing
hood is rusted cinnamon, latched over chrome priming cocks,
one for each cylinder. Every board in every building here
was milled on power from that old car, out of timber cut here
too. Even shingles. It's been here since 1925, winters piling
onto its forehead like a mother's hands. It's weathered them
like a son. Just because it hasn't been run since 1956 is no rea-
son to think it won't run now: waves have traveled thousands
of miles to give us small gifts; pine seeds have waited years to
be asked.

SNOWLIGHT

When my sister was small, Father carried her everywhere in a woven pack basket. Once he killed a deer with her strapped to his back. She moved and spoiled his first shot, and the deer ran off with one shattered hind leg. They ran two miles, stopping to shoot six times. My sister finally stopped screaming but she says her ears still ring.

My parents never said a word one way or another, but on the day before her husband died, my grandmother swears on the souls of saints she heard a banshee. Her sister, Ruth, heard it; but my sister and I were too young to be listening.

When she heard the cry, Grandmother was braiding a rug from colored rags and scraps of cloth. Her rugs began in the center and wound outward until they grew almost too large for rooms. They covered her lap and flowed to the floor, so that, to a child, she looked like the white peak of a mountain.

When Ruth shot herself, Father wrapped her body in one of my grandmother's rugs. When he returned from town, he hung the rug, like a salted hide, on the back fence. He left it there, between the tool shed and forge, for twenty years. Now it's little more than a spot on the fence, the gray boards bleached white.

Father says the worst thing is a windless December night with no moon, no stars, just snowlight glowing in through the windows, lighting the path to the springhouse. He says his ears ring so loud he can't sleep, and he thinks of the boot hammer in the shed, lying by the fenceposts; or the ring of steel on the anvil, someone forging hinges.

WITHOUT SAYING

what a small sky for so much snow; what little snow for so much ground; what looks bigger when it's farther away; you could look across the land here and think there wasn't water for a hundred miles, not see the canyon. But you'd hear it if you were close, the water like a slow explosion. I threw my mother's ashes down there, and some of them rose, too, in the wind.

Every once in a while he likes to blow up something. He loads his coat pockets with dynamite sprouting fuses. Once he set charges under the outhouse. It went up in one piece and came apart as it came down. He would crimp blasting caps to fuses with his teeth, caps inside his mouth. Once he blew windows out of the house.

Winter mornings my mother went out with ashes from the stove. First the birds went up, juncos and jays, then the snow went up in the wind, and wood ashes went up from my mother's hand in the snow and birds, and she looked up too. Nothing goes without saying. Her hem was wet, her shawl was blue.

My father lies on top of his grave, waiting to go off, waiting for a rainstorm falling into the shape of a single tree. His hat is the cloud his head is in, blown through at the peak; the wind wants to be taken into consideration.

(28)

A POEM FROM BOULDER RIDGE

The skeleton of a tepee stood on Boulder Ridge in the winter of 1950. The first year Lyle wintered on Sheep Creek with his brothers, sister and mother was 1937 and the dried elk hides still hung from the lodgepoles like the shirt of a starved man. A wind was eating his clothes. Rain licked the bones clean.

In the year I was born it fell and was covered by branches. By now it has sunk into the earth like goose down into snow.

A family of renegade Utes had left the reservation and come home to hunt where their fathers had taught them hunting. They died in the first winter, but I still feel them here, perhaps in the wood of an old ponderosa, their faces grown into pine boles: round-eyed, round-mouthed masks. Lyle's family is here too, who fell from him one after another.

Lyle's mother was a water witch for arrowheads. She showed the children where to look, near the petroglyphs on Sand Creek, or at Bull Mountain Spring. We found a few chips and scrapers, but the perfect points seemed to grow beneath her fingers as she stooped to pick them up. She peered into them and turned them over like names.

She said you have to listen to find a good arrowhead. It lies on top of the gravel and hisses with patience. You must look with eyes like flint. You pick it up, almost touching the hand that held it last, that gave it flight. You turn it over in your palm. It is like opening the door to a warm house. Someone is passing through it as if it were made for him, as if he made it.

FATHERS AND INDIANS

The mountain Utes who lived here burned these ridges to save them from settlement by whites. Like a jealous father who crops his daughter's hair to spare her the advances of vulgar young men, it was all they could do. It wasn't enough.

You can still see a few of the old trees, pitch-hardened, fire-hardened spars, standing dead and branchless for a hundred years. Once this whole country was covered with trees that size. They don't bend or break like living pines: the wind cracks and widens to let them in.

You can see them sometimes huddled together, sometimes alone like single masts in an ocean of spruce, sometimes high on open slopes in lines like somnambulists on a stair. A stair with too few steps, it doesn't reach.

Had they not been destroyed, they would not be remembered. The ones left standing remind us of the fallen, remind us there are forests of empty sleeves, tunneling into the sky.

TOTEM

Riding a '23 Farmall round and round on a hot afternoon, I always think of the dead spruce spar on the ridge behind the house. From here it pierces the skyline, asking for it, like a column of smoke. It must be a full hundred feet taller than anything living. But start up the hill and it disappears behind the smaller pines.

Why in all these years it hasn't caught a hot one and burned the whole mountain, God might have called an easy miracle. It stands bright against the sky, as if it had turned to quartz.

But I'd rather pull my hat down and watch the teeth of the hay rake making windrows, turning the meadow into a patch of corduroy, or see the iron wheels sink into the dough of the peat bog and imagine driving on the moon.

Each December I decide to cut it down. It takes till noon on snowshoes just to top the ridge, where I climb a tree for a glimpse of the spar. I walk too long, climb another and see it somewhere else, as if the forest were moving it around.

I return home in the early dark. Perhaps I see some elk or a couple of fool hens. I decide death by fire is reassuring to a forest. This year I didn't try to find the snag. This year, everything that died, died twice.

MAKING HAY AND FUNERALS

Sun comes late to the sheltered places. Any August morning she could have looked from her kitchen window, across garden rows, to the meadow. She'd have seen her son brushing frost from the tractor seat. She'd have seen his cigarette smoke suspended in air and might have thought the tractor like a barge, low in water, laboring upstream.

In winter four feet of snow could fall in a night. Any morning she could have watched the wind raising plumes into the air the way we used to believe the soul rises. Once the biggest elk they'd ever seen stood by the garden fence, wind ruffling his winter coat. The son took his rifle out to the porch. She saw the bullet hole snap open and stare.

All the neighbors came around for funerals and for haying. The women in the kitchen surrounded her like blankets. The men outside, standing or squatting in a circle, considered. After lunch, everyone seemed sleepy in the afternoon sun. Work was like a dream of work. The women wore bonnets, the men rolled cigarettes. Her husband, both her eldest sons, her only daughter: all their funerals were the same.

At night the men drank, traded songs or stories, and slept. She might have lain awake on any of those nights, listening to her last son's breathing. She might have told herself it would never stop and pulled the elk robe up over her ears. She might have remembered that collapse, how it was like an afterthought.

(33)

HOMESTEADER

From the section mark back of the meadow, straight north to the river, the telephone lines and snakefence run together. The split rails cross as if they were prayerful. Deer jump over, gray wolves slide beneath.

In the kitchen a man lights a match. A basin of water with soap and whiskers keeps moths from the lamp flame. They paddle in circles and are faithful. There are places for these men, all the same man, to drift down alone: the tie hack, the water witch, the drover, the builder of houses according to stars.

Wind in the lodgepoles is like the good son who combs his mother's hair. She talks to him steadily: about the six-pound hammer in love with the anvil, about their issue of hinges; something about the grindstone, the telephone wire, snowshoe tracks to the river and traplines lost under ice. She tells him how we sing and cry, lie down in the distance and think we sleep.

Mouthpiece, earpiece, crank handle and wire, the phone reaches to the only other man in forty miles. By the end of December the line is down from the weight of snow or the elk walking through on high drifts. The snow leans in like bad advice, eyes take on a more distant shade, the stars brighten accordingly.

(34)

Every time it snows again it's like his body filling. A wire runs in and breaks under drifts. The man picks up the earpiece and listens. It clicks and rushes. The broken wire end is like a nerve in the snow. It's a conversation with the way things are.

STRINGERS FOR THE BRIDGE

Wild mountain roses bloom in the ditches, the smell of sagebrush recurs. A single peak hovers to the north, barely visible. You have to believe in it to see it, and it *is* there: enough distance to make that difference. Small animals scatter like dice. Today we cut stringers for the bridge.

The chain saw gurgles, sputters, screams: we feed it. Ants still nest in the first tree's trunk. Cells in the body look like that, their contents mathematical and red. They bleed from the stump as I cut. They spill out and drench the chain and I press harder, as if I belonged.

I was nine when you first took me logging. We chose the straightest timber for the new barn. You taught me to use the short-handled ax, to keep it honed, to stand always on the side opposite the branches being trimmed. We went home early when a log rolled toward you and the chain saw notched your shin. You said you were ok, lucky, as we walked back to the truck and your boot filled.

Could I dig my toes into the years of needles and remain motionless long? These pine leaves fall into themselves a little confused. Like compass needles, each has an opinion of which way to go. How are they to know the map is already a wheel?

UTAH GHOST TOWN

Not to mention what was written all over them, not to mention grief, which is our own invention, all these mining towns blew in on the same hot wind and settled over the Rockies like pages from the morning news. Here the graveyard folk are mostly children, whose deaths came early on in the stories of these towns.

There are deer tracks, leaf-shaped, on the graves, and aspen leaves in the lake's palm, like money. The sky is a doubtful umbrella above the hill where the graves are, unlike the umbrellas mothers twirled on Sunday visits.

Their children must have been like gold in the bottom of a well, for they dressed in black and stood by the graves—absolute windmills—yes, and all they saw high up were white wings, those flights of pelicans disappearing into the updrafts like bits of paper, blank. And all they saw beyond the hill was land till the sky comes down.

III

for Jorie

AS IF.

I thought it took
A redtail hawk
To make hunger
Look so easy.
As if
It was your first time with me,
You lay awake all night,
Though your clothes
Went right to sleep
Like man's best friend
When you slipped
Into that other landscape.
As if the steam iron
Could dream
Of being a whale,
Becalmed in sea-wrinkles,
The distance
(Such a lonesome cowboy)
Only shrugged
And walked away.
How were you to know
What passions
Stood on their toes
For a better look
When you brushed your hair
From your forehead—

They were undone!
The vacant sun
Has better manners
Than anyone.
When you rose
In the first, slender light,
It touched your shoulder—
But only a little—
As if to say,
Excuse me, you dropped this,
Having risen all night to see you.

FOR REMEMBERING HOW TO LIVE
WITHOUT YOU

Your loneliness and mine
Added together
Make one ingenuous loneliness.

No one will believe this but you.
When you were here it rained each night.
Each morning found you

Beached against me like an irrefutable ark.
Vast, self-conscious island,
You said with eyes closed.

When you left, your pairs
Of slight nocturnal sighs went with you.
I listen to my ears ring now,

The sound of me getting nowhere.
Though I'm telling you there are mountains so distant
It hurts to look.

If there are two kinds of loving,
As everybody thinks he knows,
Two kinds of dying,

Then one of each is easy,
Like the sadness that weds us.
There are two ways to be alone:

One is filled with sunlight
And the yellowing aspen turn it, by alchemy,
Into themselves.

A DISCRETE LOVE POEM

This is for you, with your umbrella,
Your suitcase stuffed with roadmaps,
And the fatal blouse unbuttoned.

This is not for your precarious bedroom.

I couldn't help but notice
As several of your possessions assumed false identities:
The clock, for instance,
And your mother's portrait.

I couldn't keep my eyes off that space between your breasts,
A tract of liberated ground.

And later, when the bed sank
Like an earthen raft in the middle of a field, well . . .

Just the same,
This is for that night your body was neither here nor there.

THE STONE'S THROW

Tell me something. I don't care what.
Tell me despair is a dress that opens;

The nail, doubtless, is driven straight down
Into the twisted cedar post.

Say death is listening at the door.

Tell me how, between opposites, to tell
The relative from the absolute;

Why the creek sobs out at the start of spring,
Though the spring sun, among stars, is undistinguished.

Paper rose, stone's throw: show me the smallest necessities
Joining hands to complete the world.

THE LONGEST DISTANCE BETWEEN
TWO POINTS

You know this already.
I stood without warning and wandered around.

The same air hangs in the house till after the auction.
Who doesn't live before his time?

The trotlines cross from bank to bank:
Pulled downstream like apron strings,
Certain catgut lines with hooks,
Certain trout, yet uncaught.

Inside one, one blue-tail fly
And a drop of fisherman's blood.

Maybe you watch from an attic window
And think of me
As your breath on the glass comes between us.

Maybe you walk through a park, embracing
One tree after another.

Maybe you have the feeling of having been gone a long time.
Now that you're missing the harvest is this:

Light fails, wind falls back,
The earth is saved in the heart's cellardark.

LULLABY IN PRAISE OF DEATH

You are pretending to adjust the roses;
I pretend I'm sitting down.

Love, everything is a deal.
The grass doesn't mind, the magnolia leaps,

We kill the stars
(And other things) by naming them.

Ideas struggle passionately against thoughts,
The magnolia leaps.

God's old clothes, the northern lights,
Are not explanation enough,

And the instinct to praise is
Sometimes accompanied by a ridiculous dream:

Loneliness surrenders in the olive grove.
Under the glass table,

Under the night sky which resembles the table
Because covered with blossoms,

You were well hidden!
Your green or blue-green dress

Was cut from the unqualified flag
Which falls easily and is never defeated.

(48)

FOOL'S ERRAND

Alone, like a feather in the air,
An occasional sadness the weather knows
Comes to earth as a bend in the road.

The winter is at its most instructive
As other sadnesses fall
Across the democracy of objects.

Those that aren't shy
Introduce themselves—
Fool's Errand, Clowns of Anguish—

The Equitation of Beautiful Young Girls
Is an exemplary sadness,
As is The Whale's Parasol.

I want to part company
With linear extent,
Congenital heartbreak,

Where the raven goes and snow comes from.
I want distance washed clean,
Unencumbered by facts;

The red cactus flower
To slip into my shirt at dusk
And be the heart's boat.

I want Clowns of Anguish to raise the sail,
And a white handkerchief
Waving from shore.

LEMON ODE

for Neruda

Charmless and strange
At the same time,
The lemon can be opened
To interpretations,
Can encourage dispute,
Ignore abuse, absolve itself
From doubt.
(Never doubt the lemon!)

Solemnity can be forgotten
Like an apricot
Wrapped in newsprint
But not the lemon!
The lemon is always evident,
Elegant, elemental,
Swimming in clarity,
Washed in kitchen-light.

Is the lemon an oboe
On its way to an island
Because you say so?
Only the lemon
Can imagine its own precision,
Though the undecided lemon
Is more precise.

(51)

The lemon, audacious,
Drips on the barometer,
Occupies a chair.
The lemon,
As it grows, reaches.

The lemon, reckless,
Thinks, suffers,
Hopes and constantly recites,
Like the cousin
Who reminds you of a saint.

The lemon, as it burns, overflows.
The lemon, which is sour,
Makes demands.

ODE TO THE BROWN PAPER BAG

Mystery joins things together.
                    —Vallejo

Let's be more specific.
For instance, the brown paper bag.
We must not say the night is black.
Behind the night is what is black.
The bag is candid and opaque.
Consider the women with identical eyebrows,
Humiliated in the market.
Without a brown bag,
Everyone knows their brands of napkin.
And what of husbands if they are sent?
They blush at the check-out girl,
The boys in white aprons.
How can they face the streets home?
But give them a brown paper bag,
Everyone thinks they've bought an ant farm
Or a box of soap.
Mystery joins things together:
Potatoes and oranges,
Lots of oranges,
A few potatoes.
A loaf of bread is friendly as a school bus
When swaddled in brown paper.

Which brings to mind
All the embarrassments
We'll never fit into a small mysterious bag.
And we are diminished for this.

ROSARY OF CONSPIRACIES

for Stuart

On one hand, the connivance of symmetry, analogy, the heart.
Opposing this, the conspiracy of coincidence, surface,
Ellipsis, the intrigue of mismatched socks.

Is anyone else as confused as I am? It's unlucky
To be in the middle. Even my black suit is oxymoronic.
There's a conspiracy of truth, one of confusion, confederacies

Of process and music. There is watercress
In the millrace, lots of it.
The saw blade's teeth conspire to divide the tree.

The mother, though dead, is wearing her most beautiful dress.
She plans to lie down all the time now.
There's a conspiracy of son and daughters and father.

They go over each other and over the dead
Like a rosary. The mother will not concur
For death is self-devotion.

No wonder the relatives are sad.

HOW THEY GO ON

The otherwise beautiful girl
With eyes closed
Is not exactly sleeping.

A revery of dust
Obscures the photographs,
Endures the unendurable furniture.

If not to wake her,
If not, softly,
To ask what is left

Under this last, most oceanic circumstance,
The relatives lean in one by one,
As if she might tell them

How it is.
Her ears are more like seashells now,
Where those who loved her

Bend to listen, listen,
And move on,
The same as if they heard and understood.

ANOTHER STORY

I always thought you favored the bride
Of Arnolfini, though I look nothing like him

And would never wear his hat.
They hold hands, as lovers will,

But hers is turned upward in his
As if he is showing us

That it is empty. Her left hand tells
Another story, resting on her belly

Full with child. They are almost floating
Inside their clothes. They more than float

In the mirror, or between two mirrors.
As is often the case in such matters,

One of the mirrors is really a door
Where a second couple stands, smaller and less clear,

Though similar, asking to be us
For as long as we stay here.

ODE TO SIGNIFICANCE

Implications arrive in unfamiliar places:
Invading the finespun unbelievable

Down of your arm,
Moving over to accommodate a few trees
(Though each one is

And is dying to tell
An irrelevant version of the river),

Converting them to a noisy green,
A zephyr is not unlikely.
Sweet dreams

Like sailing into wind
No longer seem equivocal,

And leverage is a property
We aspire to deserve.
If we opened our eyes

That would make two of us, and yet,
Not so—

Inside the knife's edge, the cut
Occupies itself
In study of the obscure.

(58)

The truth considers turning back.
I forget who you are,

Since I love you.
But when you say,
It's the wind explains the weather vane,

I think I see what you mean.

FUGUE FOR A DROWNED GIRL

It is the time of evening that promises miracles to anyone who will believe them. People come out to their porches to see what it's like disappearing. Without regret they move around to the other side. Animals come down to water. The time of evening when trees on the edge of the forest might step into the clearing. Riverstones rub together with a sound like the turning of locks, or like bells, held tightly in both hands.

The wind comes up from the pasture as if looking for someone or thinking of the sea. Shadows of clouds ascend the canyon walls: huge trees growing hundreds of feet and disappearing in smoke. The wind has searched the riverbed down to the coast. It has returned with its arms full of branches.

Each night the sun goes down looking more and more like the moon. Each night the sound of bells moving away. Each night the moon comes up looking more and more like the only way out. Surely no one suspects her weeping. No one suspects her sadness as she thinks of the smallness of the sea, or of cattle returning from pasture. There are rows of glass jars filled with moonlight and the sound of bells approaching.

Without encouragement, without being asked, a little blood has joined the water. Children rush into the schoolyard. Late sunlight fills the high clouds. Surely no one suspects her weeping. The river looks the same. People drink it and bathe in it. They comb it into their hair. Her flesh by now is the color of silt. Her bones might be willow sticks. Fish swim into her hair. One by one the lights in her nails go out.

IV

GETTING A WORD IN

Very sad,
Having to
Come out of nowhere,

The rain
We've been waiting for
Is waiting too.

Trees,
By now,
Have had enough daylight.

They'd like,
Please,
To sleep it off.

If nothing
Else, nothing
Else.

Behind our backs
Things mean themselves.
Violins crack

From wanting to exist.
It's hard, getting a word in.
I'm waiting

To arrive inside my clothes,
If nothing else,
Willing

To be (having to
Come out of nowhere)
Very sad.

TO A FRIEND I CAN'T FIND

What about this, after all.
How does it follow?
I rent a converted garage
With shower curtains on a pipe
To divide the room in two.
I have a photograph of you
Like a grave
That I look into.
When we still lived in Colorado,
Sometimes you were happy
Without meaning it.
My sister is still in love with you.
I live in the South. I do a job. It rains.
When I let myself down,
It's easy,
And no one's left out.
The old landlord is a real goner;
I think he crossed over
And forgot to die.
He smells like piss and comes to say good-bye
Each afternoon before his nap,
And again at night.
Death can be embarrassing
When it's less than fatal.
This morning when he came over
Asking for a shave,

A starling hung from the window screen,
Like a convict on the fence,
And looked in.
Its feathers were covered with ice.
I soaped the old man's jaw
And the chain-link creases in his neck,
And I cut him once, a little.
He was alive one more time and trying
For the hang of it.
I know he'll die without meaning it.
At dusk the starlings swarm in
Like rivers of starvation.
Their dry-axle noise
Flows past the open door and eddies
In a few trees. They mean something.
They follow. They set each other off
Like fire in a good wind.
Well enough
Is never left alone;
My sister still loves you.
And you must know this, too:
After the flood
The living started digging out.

RAINSHADOW

If only we could agree that the worst isn't bad,
That only the means remain of the end,
Then the ghost we give up, the believable,

Would long have outlived its usefulness.
My disintegrating father likes to imagine
The family dead live on

In the branches of a sugar pine
On the mesa, by the springhouse.
His naming the improbable invites the impossible.

My father lives in rainshadow.
He keeps a porcelain cup in a branch, like a nest,
To taste the springwater when it's coldest;

Such reasonable furniture becomes us.
If the spring is strong in drought,
We take it on faith the tree is why.

When my father, like water, lies down in the shade,
I'll know where to find the empty cup.
I'll open a window and turn on the lights;

It will look like someone is home.

HERMITS

The more I see of people, the more I like my dog.
And this would be good country if a man could eat scenery.

The lake's ice gives light back to the air,
Shadows back to water.

In wet years the land breathes out,
And a crop of limber pines jumps into the open
Like green pioneers.
In dry years
Beetles kill them with roadmaps
Under the skin.

The land breathes in.
The sun goes down,
And the whole sky cracks like rivermud in drought.

A few trees make it each time,
As if some tide carried them out, away from the others.

They say a tree that falls in timber
Goes down in good company:
Snow drifts in and it all goes soft.

They say a ghost is a ghost
That doesn't know it's dead yet.

(68)

Those limber pines die standing, lightning-struck, wind
   broke,
And enough good pitch
For a hermit's winter.

The cabin stood; the man was long dead.
Packrats nested in the firewood,
And a crowd of medicine bottles held forth on the shelf.

When hermits die
They close their eyes. They never hear
The parson sermonize how somewhere
There is hope where no hope was.

Tanglefoot,
Dead-On-Your-Feet,
A chance to be alone for a chance to be abandoned,
Everything is lost or given.

Hermits never know they're dead till the roof falls in.

THAT FALLING WE FALL

That falling we fall, dying we rise
Are the descant pleasantries of terror.
Circumstance leaves us standing with flowers.

Everything sufficient is invented.
What is said, therefore, must be
Taken to heart and taken back:

Blue whales
Going under, the gesture of their tails
Says *amarylis*,
Elegantly and too late; beautiful women,
Ugly women, the grace of God,

Joy, no joy; the dead,
Their arms raised like violin bows
About to begin, begin to sway slowly together.

My mother was friendly, they will like her.
They will comfort her.
They will tell her this
Will never happen again,

This will never happen again.

THREE SONGS OF THE ONE-MAN BAND

Because they long for bodies, three saints
Run wind-sprints through a city which exists. It is raining.
They race over umbrellas
Like the sound of three bells.
The unhoped-for (keep this in mind)
Is upon us.
The saint with fists made of roses
Calmly aspires, wins every time.

*

Because they will die surrounded by water,
Venetian children wear three kinds of embroidered stockings.
Their shoes are made to float or be filled with flowers.
They chase after the beggar, the one-man band;
Their mothers stand on corners holding bouquets.

*

Because friends, by turns, are saying goodnight,
The sentimental boatman weeps openly—
Three handkerchiefs full of tears—
And no one will sit on his lap.
The drowning boat has something to tell us.
It is not joking.
Its reflection, indivisible,
Conforms to a vagrant wave.

(71)

CONSIDERATION OF THE SPHERE

Suppose for a moment you emerge on the frontier of laughter.
Every laugh, silly or cruel, stands like timber,
Branches impatient for a squall.

Assess the importance of this fragrance, obscure,
Unforgettable, unplaceable:
Not quite the halter left on a mule,
Hobbled in the rain.

Examine a certain shrub, laden with pods,
Each a miniature coffin.
Allow for each seed, a lace fan, falling coyly down.

Think of the way you whistle
As you pour kerosene on your shadow;
How it leaps up, bright in the afternoon.

Remember the story of the Inca king
Who covered his body with gold dust before dawn,
Rowed to the lake's sacred center.
As the sun struck him he dove
And rose up what he was.

Consider what is in us
Without us.

WIDOW OSBORNE

The widow pulled the shades one day
And that was it. The world slipped
Her mind, the house
Slipped its moorings and drifted out.
Shall we say the widow
Knows better than to go away?

Her house is poormouthed, daunted,
Clapboard-curled and trying to remember
The last flecks, like sparks, of yellow paint.
The foundation is dry masonry
Of stones annoyed with their neighbors.
Just the place

For a widow that likes to scare boys
Who fish below her house at night
Where the creek rolls down through uncut hay
Like widowsleep,
And steal the icicles from her porch in winter.
The house buckled in till the eaves touched ground,

A child's clumsy hands
Collapsing on a moth.
All you can see from the county road
(You'd never know she was alive)
Is the big tin roof,
Like a window in the green side-hill.

On the other side of the world,
Crickets fish for sadness in chokedamp air,
And the sun eases into its weary admission
That things are better here,
Green fire in the tallest pines,
The widow in her bath.

NAVIGATION

Evergreens have reasons
For stopping where they do,
At timberline or the clean edge
Of sage and prairie grass.
There are quantities of wind
They know they cannot cross.

They come down from the tundra
On waves of ridges and stop,
Staring out over open country,
Like pilgrims on the shore
Of an unexpected ocean.
The sky is still the sky, they know;
It won't understand ordinary language.

Meet my mother, twice removed,
Who could tell the time from stars.
She said everything is its own reward,
Grief, poverty, the last word.
Evening was her favorite time
And she walked along the shore of trees,
Carrying herself as if afraid
She might give herself away.
She called this being quiet.

Just inside the treeline, out of the wind,
Father built a handrail along the path.

She'd stand there like a sailor's wife
And stare at the high plains as dark came on.
She said mountains might be islands
But the sky is still the sky.
She'd wait for the ranch lights
On the prairie to come out
Like a fallen constellation.
She said waiting is its own reward,
The lights are only reasons.

CACHE LA POUDRE

The whole world
(Which you said I was
To you)
Thought it might lie down a minute
To think about its rivers.
It puts the case to you,
Admitting nothing,
The way rapids speculate
On the topic of stones.

The farmers on the Poudre should have known
From snuff-tin rings worn into their pockets:
Matter is a river
That flows through objects;
The world is a current
For carrying death away.
Their wooden fenceposts rotted fast in the bog
So they quarried stone posts from nearby bluffs.
You can guess what they looked like;

The worst of it was
They meant it.
Rivers neither marry,
Nor are they given in marriage;
The body floats
Face down in the soul;
The world turns over.

Those gritstone fences sank out of sight
Like a snowshoe thrown in the river.
The whole world
(Of human probability)
Lay under that hawk we found,
Face down, wings spread,
Not so much
Flying into it,
As seizing its double in the snow.

About the Author

James Galvin is a young poet whose work has appeared in numerous magazines, including *The New Yorker*, *The American Poetry Review*, and *Antaeus*. He was educated at Antioch College and the University of Iowa. In 1977 he was a winner of *The Nation*/Discovery Award, and in 1978 was the recipient of a grant from the National Endowment for the Arts. He lives in Trinidad, California, and teaches at California State University, Humboldt.